Hydrogen Peroxide:

Uncover the Secret Health & Beauty Benefits of Hydrogen Peroxide

Table Of Contents

Introduction

I want to thank you and congratulate you for downloading the book *"Hydrogen Peroxide: Uncover the Secret Health & Beauty Benefits of Hydrogen Peroxide."*

This book contains proven steps and strategies on how to become a truly knowledgeable consumer in using one of the best natural substances that is hydrogen peroxide or H2O2. You can use it for multiple purposes and enjoy multiple benefits as well.

Here's an inescapable fact: you will need the information presented in this book to:

- Determine the right concentration level and grade of hydrogen peroxide to use depending on your purpose. For instance, using it to water edible plants require that you choose 35% food grade H2O2, while using it to disinfect your countertop allow you to use the 3% pharmaceutical grade H2O2 solution.

- Apply and administer the solution properly, the amount of which depends on your purpose. You will also realize that only the food grade H2O2 is safe for internal use, but you need to exercise care and caution for its ingestion. For external use, H2O2 is perhaps the best replacement for chemical-based products that can increase the amount of toxins in your body.

If you do not increase your awareness and understanding of how to use hydrogen peroxide, you will definitely miss out on the multiple benefits you can get from it, such as but not limited to the following:

- Cost-effective natural remedy to maintain your personal hygiene and to enhance your beauty
- Safe cleansing and disinfectant that will kill bacteria and other pathogens that normally thrive in the kitchen
- A natural treatment and cure for ailments
- Practical and effective gardening solution

It's time for you to become an amazing H2O2 beneficiary. Read the content of the book and use it as your handy guide. This e-book does not intend to replace any suggestions, advises, or recommendations of your health practitioner.

Chapter 1: What is Hydrogen Peroxide

Hydrogen peroxide or H2O2 is a chemical combination of hydrogen and oxygen in a ratio of 2:2. It is also often referred to as hydrogen peroxide solution. This is because it is usually available as a solution formulated with water to prevent unstableness and to reduce its toxicity.

As a less concentrated aqueous solution, hydrogen peroxide works effectively and safely as an antiseptic and disinfectant. Often, you will find it in clinics as part of the cleansing routine and treatment of minor injuries such as cuts and abrasions. It is also commonly used as a bleaching agent.

Benefits and Uses

Aside from killing microbes and inhibiting them from spreading and harming your body, hydrogen peroxide has several other benefits and uses. Here are some of the big ones grouped and categorized as the following:

- Hygiene
- Cosmetics
- Kitchen
- Ailments
- Garden

Considered by many as one of the super substances, hydrogen peroxide is an interesting miracle. Testimonies are everywhere regarding its value and importance, and several studies provide the evidence and proof of its capability as multi-purpose natural remedy with countless of uses and benefits.

However, there are also those that denigrate this "super substance" and claim that it can be harmful to the body. Interestingly, the claim is consistent in stating that the danger of the substance occurs only upon ingestion. Would you ingest hydrogen peroxide?

Concentration Levels

To understand how safe hydrogen peroxide is, and to minimize the risk, if any, let us look into the different levels of concentration of this substance.

The concentration of hydrogen peroxide is expressed in terms of percentage or volume. The ones you can buy from online or offline retail stores are typically in low concentrations to ensure stability and safety.

Volume

Most often than not, you will encounter hydrogen peroxide with concentration or strength that is expressed in either volumes or percentage. The table below shows the volumes usually available in the market and the corresponding percentage.

Volume	Percentage
10	3
20	6
30	9
40	12

If expressed in terms of volumes, you will know the amount of oxygen that is released from 1 ml of H_2O_2. For example, 1 ml of 30 volumes releases 30 ml oxygen. On the other hand, percentage represents the amount of pure H_2O_2 present in the solution. Example, 100 ml of 9% hydrogen peroxide solution contains 9 ml of pure H_2O_2 with 91ml of water.

Thus, the higher the concentration of the solution is, the greater the amount of pure hydrogen peroxide is in the solution and the more oxygen it releases. However, you will not find 100% hydrogen peroxide as it will be extremely dangerous. Most commercially available H_2O_2 are from 3% to 35% in concentration.

Grades

Aside from concentration levels, the grade of hydrogen peroxide can also determine its safety and usage. The table below shows you the various grades:

Grade	Brief Description
Food Grade	Used as an ingredient to produce food such as egg products. Food manufacturers also use it to spray the

	linings of milk packages as well as fruit juice packages. If you need to use H2O2 internally, this is the only grade that is suitable for ingestion.
Pharmaceutical/Grocery Store Grade	Is usually available in 10 volumes or 3% solution from drug stores or grocery stores. It contains stabilizers that are not edible and therefore must not be ingested. Common uses are for disinfection and may also be used as a mouthwash when diluted with two parts water (1:2)
Beautician Grade	Is not suitable for use internally. This grade is used as a bleaching or coloring agent for hair. It starts with volume 20 or 6% solution up to 40 volumes or 12% solution.
Electronic Grade	Must not be ingested. This grade is used to clean electronic parts.
Technical Grade	Contains phosphorous to counteract the chlorine in water used as solvent for the solution. It is not suitable for internal as well as household uses.
Industrial Grade	is of higher concentration and is only appropriate for industrial, manufacturing, and chemical uses or purposes. This includes using it as source of oxygen for rocket fuel.

Production

Hydrogen peroxide is produced either naturally or commercially. Below are the details on how this super substance is made.

Natural

In nature, you will find the following producers of hydrogen peroxide:

- Rain – when rainwater or even snow passes within the ozone layer, some of its molecules collect extra oxygen, thus turning H2O (water) into hydrogen peroxide (H2O2).

- Water – can also produce or convert itself into hydrogen peroxide through exposure to sunlight or air containing lots of oxygen such as with rapids or waterfall.

- Cells – of most living things including human body cells have the capability to produce hydrogen peroxide. During the metabolic process, these cells produce hydrogen peroxide as an offshoot.

Further, the human body's white blood cells and T-cells can also make hydrogen peroxide as protection against diseases.

Fresh fruits and vegetables also contain H_2O_2 naturally which contributes to the nutrients and benefits. However, the substance usually escapes during the cooking process. This is one reason why raw fruits and veggies have higher nutrient content and more health benefits than their cooked counterparts.

Commercial

However, practically all hydrogen peroxide that you know come from commercial manufacturing using the auto-oxidation process. Part of this process is to use stabilizers for all grades, except for food grade H_2O_2, making the product unfit for ingestion. This is to prevent the product to decompose.

Meanwhile, food grade H_2O_2 contains none of the stabilizers. It is the purified form of H_2O_2 and may be ingested without harming the body.

The next chapter will discuss how you can use hydrogen peroxide for hygienic purposes.

Chapter 2:   Hygiene Options for Hydrogen Peroxide

Natural Ingredient

Most oral hygiene products today contain hydrogen peroxide in its capacity either as a bleaching agent or as a disinfectant or both. This substance is a common ingredient of teeth whiteners because of its bleaching properties. Toothpastes and mouthwashes may also contain acceptable amount of H2O2 in low concentrations. H2O2 works as a disinfectant to protect the teeth and gums against plagues, inflammation, and infection.

H2O2 in dental products such as mouth rinses and toothpastes are safe and harmless as long as the products only contain small amount and in low concentrations. This is because the saliva easily breaks the substance without interference from the other ingredients present in the dental products such as fluoride. Results from one study show how the saliva was able to break down up to 70% of H2O2 immediately during the initial minute of tooth brushing.

Mouth Rinse

You have the option to use hydrogen peroxide as your mouth rinsing solution. Since H2O2 is a disinfectant, it can kill harmful microbes present in your mouth. Here's is how to use H2O2 as a mouth rinse safely:

What You Will Need	How to Do It
• Hydrogen peroxide 10 volumes or 3% solution	1. In a cup, create your H2O2 mouth rinse solution following the 1:2 ratio. Mix one part of hydrogen peroxide with two parts of warm water.
• Warm water • Cup or glass	2. Drink, but do not swallow, the solution. In a swishing motion, rinse your mouth with the H2O2 solution (like you would your regular mouth rinse).
	3. Make sure that you swish the solution in between your teeth. This will enable the hydrogen peroxide to pull the bacteria present and protect the health of your gums.
	4. After a minute or two of gargling, spit the solution.

Bad Breath

Bad breath is not only a sign of a possible ailment, but also an embarrassing condition. However, one way to get rid of bad breath and prevent it from coming back is to pay attention to your oral hygiene. As part of your oral hygiene, hydrogen peroxide proves to be effective in getting rid of bad breath. Here's how.

What You Will Need	How to Do It
• Hydrogen peroxide, 10 volumes or 3% solution	1. Dip your toothbrush into the H2O2 solution. Brush your tongue in a scraping motion.
• Toothbrush	2. Rinse with H2O2 solution (one part of H2O2 mixed with 2 parts of warm water).
• Warm water • Cup or glass	3. Brush your teeth using your regular toothpaste. Rinse with just water.
	4. Gargle with H2O2 solution. Be sure to spit out the liquid. Follow up with just warm water for the final rinse.

Vaginal Odor

You can create your own feminine wash to remove vaginal odor with hydrogen peroxide as your natural ingredient. Here's the recipe for your homemade vaginal odor remover.

Ingredients	Procedure
Hydrogen Peroxide 3% solution	1. Mix one part of hydrogen peroxide with three parts of water (1:3).
Water	2. Wash your vagina with the mixture.

Ear Wax

If you need to remove accumulated ear wax and prevent it to happen again, one of your best natural solutions is to use hydrogen peroxide. This natural substance has the ability to soften the wax inside your ears for easy removal thereafter. Just follow these:

What You Will Need	How to Do It
• **Hydrogen peroxide pharmaceutical grade 3% solution**	1. Wet one piece of cotton ball with H2O2 solution. Make sure that the cotton ball is all wet.
• **Towel**	2. With the towel under your head, lie on your side. Place the cotton ball slightly above your ear opening, and then squeeze.
• **Cotton Balls**	3. Let the H2O2 solution stay in your ear for about ten minutes. As the H2O2 solution gets into contact and mingles with your ear wax, you will hear bubbling sounds. It means the solution is softening the wax.
	4. Turn on the other side to let the hydrogen peroxide along with the softened wax drain.

Deodorant

To fight and prevent body odor, especially foul odor coming from the underarms, you can use hydrogen peroxide as a natural remedy. The best thing about using H2O2 is that it addresses the root of your body odor, such as getting rid of the bacteria that is causing your underarms to give off the bad odor.

Ingredients	Procedure

• Hydrogen Peroxide 3% solution	1. In a spray bottle, combine one part of hydrogen peroxide with two parts of water (1:2).
• Your choice of essential oil	2. Pour a few drops of your preferred essential oil.
• Water	3. Spray the mixture on your armpits, about five to eight sprays for each armpit.

Foot Odor

Foul odor emanating from your feet usually comes from bacteria and viruses that have chosen your feet as their home. Thus, to get rid of the foul smell permanently, you need to kill these microbes inhabiting on your feet. One of your best weapons to do so is hydrogen peroxide. Here's how to get rid of microbes.

As Footbath

Pour enough hot water to soak your feet. Make sure that the heat is enough and tolerable (the least that you want is to scorch your feet!). Pour a few drops of 3% hydrogen peroxide (food grade preferably or pharmaceutical grade), or follow this ratio: one part of H2O2 to two parts of water (1:2). You have the option to add your favorite essential oil for fragrance. Soak your feet for about five to ten minutes.

As Foot Spray

You can also use the solution of one part hydrogen peroxide, two parts water, and a few drops of essential oil as your foot spray. This comes in handy when you do not have enough time for a foot bath. Spray the solution onto your feet, let it air dry as much as possible before wearing anything on your feet.

To prevent the microbes from coming back, treat your footwear with the solution as well. You can spray the inside of your shoes with the H2O2 solution, but be cautious with footwear made of leather. This is because water and any other substance may cause some damage to leather.

In the next chapter, we shall look into how you can use hydrogen peroxide to enhance your beauty and for cosmetic purposes.

Chapter 3: Cosmetic Uses for Hydrogen Peroxide

Teeth Whitening

One of the most popular uses of hydrogen peroxide is to whiten the teeth. As mentioned in the previous chapter, most teeth whitening products today, if not all, use it as a natural ingredient to bleach the teeth and remove stains.

How it Whitens Teeth

H_2O_2 has the ability to whiten the teeth because it contains natural bleaching properties that can penetrate the teeth to remove stains and discoloration. This is also the very reason teeth whitening products use it as one of their ingredients.

Note that commercially sold products may vary in the H_2O_2 concentration they contain. This difference, in turn, determine if the products are: (1) sold over the counter; (2) prescribed by dentist for home use; or (3) exclusive for professional use that only dentists can apply the product to their patients.

For heavy stains and discolorations, it may take a number of months, usually three (3) months, to lighten or whiten the teeth. Dental health experts agree that reputable teeth whitening products containing H_2O_2 do no harm to the teeth.

There are instances of side effects, but these are minor and temporary. The common side effects are: (1) increased sensitivity of the teeth; and/or (2) irritation of the mouth. However, with the latter, the experts find that what triggers the irritation is not the use of the teeth whitener, but the tool to apply it such as with the dental tray or mouth guard. Further, side effects only happen from accidental swallowing of the whitener that it causes gastrointestinal upsets.

Natural Teeth Whitener

You may also create your own natural teeth whitener using hydrogen peroxide as your whitening agent. Here is the recipe:

Ingredients	Procedure
• Hydrogen Peroxide 3% solution • Baking soda	1. In a mixing bowl, combine one (1) teaspoon of baking soda with two drops of H_2O_2 to form a paste. 2. Apply the baking soda-hydrogen peroxide paste into your toothbrush and proceed brushing your teeth.

It is important that after brushing your teeth with hydrogen peroxide-baking soda paste, you should rinse your mouth thoroughly with fresh clean water to remove any residue. Avoid swallowing the mixture, as it may cause you stomach upsets.

Clear Skin

If you want to clear your skin from blemishes, age spots, and other impurities, or if you want to lighten your skin, then you have a natural solution in hydrogen peroxide. Choose low level of concentration or the 3% (10 volumes) variant.

What You Will Need	How to Do It
• Hydrogen peroxide pharmaceutical grade 3% solution	1. Soak your cotton ball into your hydrogen peroxide solution: one part of hydrogen peroxide mixed with two parts of water (1:2).
• Cotton Balls	2. Gently rub your blemished skin with the soaked cotton ball.
	3. Only apply the hydrogen peroxide solution to a specific area. Be careful and prudent not to apply the solution to your entire body without consulting your skin care specialist.
	4. Before you apply the H2O2 solution, be sure to test it first to determine your skin's reaction to the substance.

Hair Bleach

Professional hair bleaching is a costly treatment. If you wish to lighten your hair color, but you do not have the bucks to spare for it, then a practical alternative is to do it yourself using H2O2.

Here is a step-by-step procedure on how to do it.

What You Will Need	How to Do It
• Hydrogen peroxide pharmaceutical grade 3% solution	1. Clip some of your hair strands and tie them together. You will use these strands to perform a test that will give you a preview of your new hair color after undergoing the lightening process.
• Squeeze bottle	2. Wash your hair. Let your hair dry a little and then comb it to remove the tangles.
• Hand gloves	
• Comb	3. Wear your hand gloves. Create your hair lightening solution by mixing two parts of hydrogen peroxide with two parts of water. Transfer the solution into your squeeze bottle.
• Towel	
• Pure coconut oil	4. Spray the solution onto your damp hair. Make sure that the solution does not reach your scalp. Wrap your head with a towel to prevent the solution from reaching your face.
	5. You may choose to lighten specific hair strands instead of lightening your entire hair.
	6. Let the solution stand in your hair for about 10 to 15 minutes, after which you must rinse your hair thoroughly.
	7. You may repeat the process to achieve your desired lightening.
	8. Gently massage your hair and scalp with pure coconut oil to prevent drying. The oil will work as your natural conditioning agent.

Disinfectant for Your Beauty Tools

It is important and necessary to use clean and sanitized tools as they come in contact with your skin. Thus, you have to make sure that you thoroughly clean and disinfect them, as they can collect microbes such as bacterial and viruses with repeated use.

Here are two of the most frequently used tools that require regular cleaning and disinfecting:

1. Toothbrush
2. Comb

Tooth Brush

The toothbrush that you use to whiten your teeth collects bacteria and viruses as you use it. Thus, in between uses, you are better off soaking your toothbrush in a glass filled with hydrogen peroxide solution, one part H_2O_2 two parts water or for stronger disinfection; you can follow the 1:1 ratio, one part H_2O_2 to one part water.

Comb

Dirt accumulates in your comb over time. With dirt build-up, microbes may decide to make your comb their dwelling place. Therefore, it is best that you clean and disinfect your comb from time to time and not to wait for dirt to accumulate.

Here is how to clean and sanitize your comb:

What You Will Need	How to Do It
• Hydrogen peroxide pharmaceutical grade 3%- 6% solution	1. Fill your basin with warm water. Add a few drops of your dishwashing soap.
• Dishwashing soap • Basin	2. Make sure that your comb is free from hair strands. Soak it in the basin filled with soapy water for about 5 minutes. This will soften the dirt for easy removal. Proceed with the dirt removal thereafter. You can scrub the comb using an old toothbrush.
• Old toothbrush • Hand towel	3. Rinse your comb thoroughly and place it on the hand towel to dry.

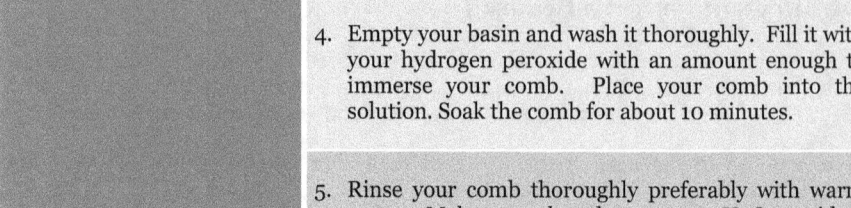

4. Empty your basin and wash it thoroughly. Fill it with your hydrogen peroxide with an amount enough to immerse your comb. Place your comb into the solution. Soak the comb for about 10 minutes.

5. Rinse your comb thoroughly preferably with warm water. Make sure that there are no H2O2 residue. Let your comb air dry on your hand towel.

So far you have learned how hydrogen peroxide is an effective natural cleansing and disinfecting agent with multiple uses for hygiene and cosmetics. In the next chapter, you will discover how H2O2 has the power to cure and prevent ailments.

Chapter 4: Ailments Cured with Hydrogen Peroxide

It will amaze you to discover that a natural substance that is normally used as a cleansing and disinfecting agent can also heal the body and cure ailments. Why don't we start with the most dreaded disease, the big C?

Anti-Cancer

The American Cancer Society lists oxygen therapy also known as hydrogen peroxide therapy as one of the alternative treatment options for cancer. Using hydrogen peroxide/ozone in small quantity and under a carefully controlled environment can be effective in treating some parts of the body and certain types of cancer.

The reason behind this is the fact that cancer cells are anaerobic that in order to thrive they need an oxygen-free environment as much as possible. Therefore, denying these cells the environment they need to survive will inhibit their growth and either stop or delay their progression and spread in the body.

The kind that can help treat certain types of cancer is 35% food grade hydrogen peroxide, the only H2O2 permitted to be taken internally. It is also important that as treatment for cancer, only professional or your physician should administer and supervise it.

If you are to use 35% food grade hydrogen peroxide as an at home treatment, the safest way to do it is through getting a warm bathe. Mix not more than one (1) cup of the peroxide into your bathtub filled with warm water. Soak for up to 30 minutes.

Gum Disease

Gum disease which includes gingivitis (inflammation of the gums) and periodontitis (serious infection that damages and destroys the bone supporting your teeth) is a serious dental health condition that you should treat with a sense of urgency.

Dental treatments are costly, but you can easily avoid the cost by benefiting from a proven treatment for gum disease. This is the hydrogen peroxide treatment. H2O2 kills microbes such as bacteria in plague that cause the disease. Remember that addressing the problem at its root is the most effective treatment that brings permanent results.

You can use H2O2 as an at home treatment for gingivitis and periodontitis. In fact, the Food and Drug Administration recognizes the ability of hydrogen peroxide to stop the progression of gum disease and to prevent it. It is most effective when you use it as part of your dental health hygiene.

Here is an effective way to include hydrogen peroxide in your dental hygiene routine. Use it as your mouth rinse. Pour about 15 ml of 3% H2O2 in your mouth. Don't worry about the foam it will make when you swish the solution since it is an indication of the solution disinfecting and killing the bacteria in your mouth including those that linger on your gums. See to it that you spit the solution and that you rinse your mouth with fresh water thoroughly to remove any residue.

Do the rinse daily until your gum health improves. When your gum heals from the disease, limit your H2O2 mouth rinse from daily to once a week or once every two weeks and follow the ratio of 1:2 or one part H2O2 to two parts warm water.

Colds & Flu

The most common ailment, colds and flu, is curable with H2O2 treatment. Fact is, Dr. Joseph Mercola considers it an exception to his one general rule of refraining from advising over-the-counter medications. He finds the treatment effective in treating upper respiratory tract infections.

Dr. Mercola has been using the treatment to his patients suffering from colds and flu. So far, the H2O2 treatment proves to deliver significant results. As early as 12 hours to 24 hours of treatment, colds and flu start to flee and his patients experience great relief from their condition.

To benefit from H2O2 as a treatment and cure for colds and flu, Dr. Mercola suggests the following steps:

1. Using 3% (10 volumes) hydrogen peroxide that you usually buy from your drug store or grocery story (you may also get it online), fill its cap with the solution. You need not dilute the solution, but if you wish to do so, you may follow the 1:1 ratio or one part H2O2 to one part of water.

2. Pour the solution into one of your ears. You may use a medicine dropper to do this, or to slowly pour the solution from the cap. You may experience the following which should not alarm you as these are normal to the treatment: (1) sparkling sound, an indicator that the solution is doing its job; and (2) a slightly stinging sensation. These will last for approximately ten minutes at the most.

3. As the sparkling and stinging sensation subside, tilt your ear to drain the solution. Repeat the process into your other ear.

According to Dr. Mercola, the H2O2 treatment for colds and flu work best when you administer it as soon as the symptoms appear. Otherwise, it may not work as effectively as it should. It is also important that whether you suffer from colds and flu or not, you continue to take good care of and strengthen your immune system as it is your body's shield and protection against diseases and infections.

Toothache

Like colds and flu, toothache is one of the most common ailments that can happen to anyone. Unlike colds and flu, the pain from a toothache can be unbearable. Colds and flu and toothache have a common denominator when it comes to treatment and cure. This is the hydrogen peroxide treatment.

Here is how you can benefit from the H2O2 solution to get rid of the pain that will last until you visit your dentist to check on your teeth.

1. The first step is to brush your teeth to make sure that there are no food particles lodged in between your teeth. Follow this up with a warm water-salt solution.

2. Next is to create your H2O2 mouth rinse. Use 3% hydrogen peroxide solution. You have at least two options here. If the pain is unbearable, use the peroxide in full strength, meaning undiluted. Just swish a capful in your mouth to drive the pain away.

   Another option is to dilute the solution following any of these ratios: 1:1 or 1:2, where you mix one part of H2O2 with one part of warm water or mix one part of H2O2 with two parts of water. Use the solution as your mouth rinse.

   Whatever option you choose to follow, be sure to spit the H2O2 solution and thereafter rinse your mouth with warm water. Avoid swallowing the hydrogen peroxide solution, as it is not recommended for ingestion.

3. For added relief, you may follow your hydrogen peroxide with either a hot or cold compress applied to the cheek where your toothache is.

Nail Fungus

Hydrogen peroxide is effective in treating nail fungal infection. This is because H2O2 deprives the fungi the environment they need to survive and thrive. Here is how you can use it to treat your nail fungal infection:

1. Use a large basin if the infection is in your feet or a small basin if it is in your hands. The basin should be able to accommodate the H2O2-water solution enough to submerge your feet or hands.

2. Fill the basin with warm water. Add 3% hydrogen peroxide. Choose any of these two ratios: 1:1 (one part H2O2 to one part warm water) or 1:2 (one part H2O2 to two parts water). For severe infection, add one part of apple cider vinegar. You may also pour a few drops of essential oil, but choose from among the oils that also disinfect such as eucalyptus, peppermint, tea tree, or red thyme.

3. Place the hand or foot affected by the nail fungus in the basin and soak for about 30 minutes. Following this, rinse your hand or your foot thoroughly with warm water. Dry your hand or foot paying attention to your nails. Repeat the process with your other hand or foot.

4. You may repeat the process for both your hands and feet up to three times daily until the infection clears.

Ear Infections

Hydrogen peroxide is a popular natural remedy for ear infections, especially those that are caused by cuts or scrapes in your ears. It can also drive away pain and heal pierced ears. Here is how to free your ears from infection using H2O2 solution.

1. Prepare the things that you will need to treat your ear infection. These are the following:

    - Hydrogen peroxide 3% solution
    - rubbing alcohol
    - bulb syringe aspirator
    - cotton balls
    - medicine dropper
    - warm water
    - clean towel

2. Position your infected ear to face the ceiling. Apply up to three drops of hydrogen peroxide to the ear using the medicine dropper.

3. You will hear foaming or bubbling in your ear which should not alarm you. It only means that the hydrogen peroxide is killing the bacteria that cause the infection. This lasts for about five minutes at the least and anywhere between 10-15 minutes at the most.

4. Tilt your head to allow the solution to drain. Repeat steps 2-4 if your other ear is infected too.

5. To prevent infection, remove earwax through the bulb syringe aspirator. Wet your cotton ball with alcohol and squeeze a tiny amount into each of your ears and then drain as usual.

There are several other ailments that hydrogen peroxide can cure that you are better off including it in your medicine cabinet at home.

Chapter 5: Kitchen Uses for Hydrogen Peroxide

You will be pleasantly surprised to discover that hydrogen peroxide can replace a lot of chemical-based products in your kitchen. You may not know it, but your usual kitchen products are toxic to your health. Replacing them with H2O2 will minimize your exposure to toxins. You will also be able to save on the cost of your kitchen products.

The primary use of hydrogen peroxide in the kitchen is as a cleansing and sanitizing agent. The kitchen is one area in your home that is attractive to microbes such as bacteria, fungi, and viruses. These microorganisms are so tiny that you will easily think that with your usual cleaning routine, they are no longer present in your kitchen.

However, they reside in almost all areas in your kitchen, especially the ones where you prepare your food. You would normally use chemical-based products such as chlorine bleach.

What you may not be conscious about is the fact that such products contain chemicals and other synthetic ingredients that are toxic to the body. They enter your body through your skin pores and with frequent exposure to these toxins; you are compromising your good health. To minimize such exposure, use hydrogen peroxide.

How to Use Hydrogen Peroxide as a Sanitizing Agent

H2O2 has the power to kill germs commonly residing in your kitchen such as Salmonella and Norovirus. It can also kill toxic germs such as E. coli and Listeria Monocytogenes that can trigger life threatening diseases.

To use H2O2 as a sanitizer, follow these steps:

1. See to it that before you proceed with sanitizing the surfaces, you clean them thoroughly. This will increase the effectiveness of the hydrogen peroxide solution to kill germs and other pathogens lurking in your kitchen.

2. Use ½ cup of hydrogen peroxide 3% solution (10 volumes), or ¼ cup of hydrogen peroxide 6% solution (20 volumes). To start using it for sanitation, pour the solution into a spray bottle.

3. Proceed spraying your kitchen surfaces, countertop, appliances such as refrigerator and microwave oven with the solution. Let the H2O2 solution sit for at least 10 minutes before you wipe it off or rinse (e.g. utensils) until no residue is left.

It is also important that in using it as a sanitizing agent, you must not dilute your hydrogen peroxide solution or mix it with other ingredients such as vinegar and baking soda.

How to Use Hydrogen Peroxide as a Cleanser

You can also use hydrogen peroxide as part of your cleaning routine in your kitchen. If this is the purpose, you can mix hydrogen peroxide with water on a 1:1 ratio or 1:2 ratios-the first digit in both ratios goes to H2O2, the second digit to water.

Follow these steps:

1. Depending on the surface, wash it with warm water and mild soap or dishwashing liquid, or wipe with clean cloth soaked in warm water and soap.

2. Rinse the surface or wipe to remove soap residue.

3. Spray the hydrogen peroxide solution on the surface for cleaning.

4. Do your final rinse to remove all traces of soap or H2O2.

5. Let the surface air dry or wipe with clean and sanitized cloth.

Surfaces for Cleaning and Sanitation

Be sure to clean the following surfaces daily and sanitize them at least once a week:

- ✓ Cutting or chopping boards
- ✓ Sinks
- ✓ Countertops
- ✓ Refrigerator
- ✓ Microwave oven
- ✓ Toaster
- ✓ Garbage bin/s
- ✓ Floor

Use hydrogen peroxide solution to disinfect the following:

- ✓ Dish scrubbers
- ✓ Rags or cleaning cloths
- ✓ Sponges
- ✓ Floor mop

Chapter 6: Garden Uses for Hydrogen Peroxide

You think you have exhausted your options for hydrogen peroxide? You will benefit much from hydrogen peroxide no matter what type of garden you have:

- Indoor or outdoor
- Garden of edible plants or non-edible plants
- Traditional gardening or modern gardening such as with hydroponics

The main function and benefit of hydrogen peroxide in gardening is the release of added oxygen that can:

- Deliver more nutrients to the plants
- Speed up their growth and improve their health
- Drive away and repel pests and insects
- Kill pathogens that can damage your plants

The succeeding paragraphs will show you how you can use hydrogen peroxide in growing and nurturing your garden.

Food for your Plants

Do you know the reason why plants seem to grow well with rainwater? The answer is hydrogen peroxide that is naturally occurring in rainwater. You cannot expect rain to happen all the time just to water your garden, but you can always simulate rainwater by combining hydrogen peroxide with tap water and sprinkle the solution onto your plants.

What You Will Need	How to Do It
• Hydrogen peroxide 35% food grade • Spray bottle • Watering can	1. Create your H2O2 fertilizer. If you are watering your plants without the use of a garden hose, i.e. potted plants, indoor plants, mix two teaspoons of H2O2 with one gallon of tap water and pour the solution in your watering can. Next is to fill your spray bottle with water and add half a teaspoon of the peroxide.
• Hand gloves	2. To protect your hands, wear hand gloves while gardening and watering your plants.

3. Proceed with watering your plants. Spray the solution on the leaves and flowers.

4. If you are to use your garden hose with a fertilizer spray attachment, just add 6 tablespoons plus two teaspoons of H2O2 for 10-gallon spray, and 13 tablespoons plus one teaspoon of H2O2 for 20-gallon spray.

Pest & Insect Repeller

Another important use of hydrogen peroxide for your garden is to drive away pests and insects that can hurt your plants. You can create your H2O2 solution and spray it on the leaves. The solution will kill the eggs and larvae and will prevent infestations.

For every gallon of water, add one tablespoon plus one teaspoon of hydrogen peroxide 35% food grade. You may also use the 3% pharmaceutical grade hydrogen peroxide to spray on non-edible plants following this ratio: for every gallon of water, add one cup of H2O2.

The solution can serve as your natural pest repeller. Be careful not to increase the amount of peroxide, as more does not always equate to better.

Seed Germination Accelerator

Hydrogen peroxide speeds up the germination of seeds. To enjoy this benefit, here is what you can do:

Soak your seeds in 3% pharmaceutical grade H2O2 solution (for non-edible plants) or 35% food grade H2O2 solution following these ratios:

- 1 cup of water, add 1.5 teaspoons of 3% H2O2 or up to 10 drops of 35% food grade H2O2

- For every gallon of water, add ½ cup of 3% H2O2 or 2 teaspoons of 35% food grade H2O2

You will also notice more sprouts since the solution will kill bacteria and other pathogens that may inhabit on the seed coat.

Hydroponics

Hydrogen peroxide is an essential element in hydroponic gardening. When poured into the tank, the solution gives off extra oxygen that strengthens the roots of the plants and increases their ability to absorb nutrients.

Along with best practices, there is the guarantee that you will grow healthier plants with the H2O2 solution. This is because:

- H2O2 kills harmful bacteria that survive in low-oxygen water tanks. One tip in determining oxygen level is to follow this rule: the warmer the water gets, the lower the oxygen level is. H2O2 increases oxygen in the water tank and stabilize water temperature to promote the growth of healthy plants.

- It prevents rotting of your plant roots. The presence of bacteria and other pathogens can cause the roots to rot. H2O2 can halt the spread of bacteria and pathogens and eliminate them to prevent them from invading your hydroponic garden.

- Hydrogen peroxide has the ability to remove impurities in the water. It can get rid of chlorine to purify the water. Chlorine and other impurities in the water can hamper or slow down plant growth. Further, plants grow well with clean and pure water.

- The solution will help your plants to absorb nutrients better. With better absorption of nutrients, your plants will grow bigger, thicker, or heavier. H2O2 also speeds up their growth and improve their health condition.

Conclusion

Thank you again for downloading this book!

I hope this book was able to help you to:

- Get to know hydrogen peroxide as a multi-purpose natural "super substance" that also brings multiple benefits.

- Learn that hydrogen peroxide comes in different volumes or percentages of concentrations and grades such as: 10 volumes or 3%, 20 volumes or 6%, 30 volumes or 9%, and 40 volumes or 12% as well as 35% food grade H_2O_2, pharmaceutical or grocery store grade, beautician grade, technical grade, and industrial grade.

- Discover proven strategies, procedures, and tips to use hydrogen peroxide as part of your personal hygiene and beauty regimen, for cosmetic purposes, as cleansing and sanitizing agent in your kitchen, to cure common ailments or as part of the treatment for certain types of cancer, and in gardening.

- How to create your H_2O_2 solution suitable for your purpose in using this natural substance.

The next step is to explore other uses and benefits of hydrogen peroxide as there are several more. You may also want to search where to get it at its most reasonable cost, especially when you have to use a lot of H_2O_2 on a regular basis such as with gardening.

Finally, if you enjoyed this book, please take the time to share your thoughts and post a review on Amazon. It'd be greatly appreciated!

Thank you and good luck!

www.ingramcontent.com/pod-product-compliance
Lightning Source LLC
Chambersburg PA
CBHW070254290526
45789CB00004B/1852